# HOW TO QUICKLY GROW YOUR INSTAGRAM FOLLOWERS

## FOR CHEFS, RESTAURANTS, FOOD BLOGGERS & INFLUENCERS

**Published by Prolific Authority Publishing**
**Copyright © 2021 by Brax Rich**

*Grateful acknowledgment is made to Ash Cash for the inspiration and motivation to write this book.*

# CONTENTS

## CHAPTER 1:

# MINDSET & MOTIVATION

**Words to work by:**

*Comparison is the thief of joy.*

*There are no losses if you learn from it.*

*Focus. One word.*

**Feed your Feed**

*Mind over matter.*

I'm sure you would agree with me when I tell you that mindset is the number one, most important tool that you will need along this journey. Actually, for most things, it's how we choose to look at the situations or opportunities that determine how high we will go.

Webster's dictionary defines mind over matter as someone's ability to control a physical condition or problem using their mind.

Before we began to dive into all of the different strategies and tricks we used to grow our Instagram page, we need to make sure that the vehicle we are driving is up to par to make it to the end of the journey; your mind.

So let's put things into perspective because as you start, you're going to see a bunch of social media accounts with hundreds of thousands of followers—tons of engagement, likes, and a bunch of fantastic posts and creative content. I want to get this clear now; it will be vital that you do not compare yourself to them. Yes, strive to be just as good as them, and you can even secretly compete with them. But remember this quote, "comparison is the thief of joy." Don't allow insecurities to drain you or rob you of your energy. Social media is a collection of energy and a collector of energy. Either you use it, or it will use you. Nevertheless, Instagram is an excellent tool for growing your brand, but only if you use it efficiently.

Secondly, I want you to understand that there are no losses if you learn from it. As we go through this process of building up your social media, you're going to try things, and it's not going to work. You're going to have expectations, and it may not turn out the way you believe it will. But that does not mean that you're losing or failing at social media. No, it simply means that you found out what does not work. As long as you learn from it and you keep going, you didn't fail. Sometimes you have to get over a speed bump or hurdle to get to the next step. By this, I mean that something you tried didn't work as expected or, shall I say, as soon as you expected. This doesn't mean you failed. It just means you're working your way through the process, and sometimes it takes a moment for people to notice. I want you to understand this as we work to grow your social media presents.

While these tips, tricks, and strategies are tried and true, everyone's audience and brand will have their differences. There's going to be some caveats that might work for you that won't work for others, and vice versa; some things might work for them, that won't work for you. So with that said, I want us to always be in the mindset that we are experimenting and trying new things through trial and error. We are filtering our way through this process and figuring out what works best for our audience and our brand's growth.

**Audience:** It's fair to say that while Walmart and Target both have similar business models, they do not serve the same audience. That will also be true for your social media presence versus your competitor's social media presence or those in the same focus or niche as you.

**Focus:** Bill Gates and Warren Buffett were at a dinner event together. Bill Gates's mother asked everyone around the table to write down the one word that they believe is the single most important factor in their success throughout life. Bill Gates and Warren Buffett both wrote down the same one-word answer. Focus.

When people think of the word focus, they often think of someone working towards one goal in mind, and this is true. However, I also want you to remember that as you go through the process of building on your social media presence. Focus is a state of flow, and flow is where the magic happens. As you grow your brand and your social media, I want you to remain focused, even throughout the daily task. In a world full of so many distractions, we can quickly lose countless hours of productivity by mindlessly scrolling through hours and hours of social media feeds.

It's nothing wrong to scroll through social media; actually, I recommend it. Stay active and engaged, especially in your niche community but remember what you're looking for and what you're here to do. Attention to detail is going to be critical to your success. It would help if you always stay mindful of your goals. You will begin to notice that you can learn or find inspiration from almost anything and everything throughout this journey.

Let's take Kobe Bryant, for example, with the famous mantra "Mamba Mentality."

The Mamba mentality is a mindset of constant self-improvement and the pursuit of your highest potential in life. Suppose you think about your social media brand from this perspective, while Kobe Bryant loved the game of basketball and played just as hard on the court as he did off the court. He also was a student of the game of life. If you have ever watched any of Kobe Bryant's interviews, he will mention that he also picked up different lessons in life that he applied to the game of basketball. I want you to do the same as you think about your brand, business, and your social media presents. There are many things to be learned from nature, relationships, and even family. You can even learn what not to do from someone who didn't figure out the right way and found failure. Remember, we are in a constant state of growth, and what works today may not work tomorrow.

So while these tips and strategies, if applied appropriately, will absolutely work for you. What's even more important is that you understand the mechanisms behind these tricks and tips. Because once you know that, even if Instagram changed its algorithms tomorrow or completely disappeared. And the next platform emerged, you will still understand people and what they want. Once you figure out the formula for growth, you will always understand what connects to your audience. Besides, you won't grow if you don't. But what's most important is that you will understand yourself and the role you fill in the world of social media.

## CHAPTER 2

# RICHES IN NICHES

Successful businesses don't fit everyone. Every successful company has a specific niche or caters to a general need or theme. It doesn't matter whether you're looking at Amazon. Walmart, Target, UPS, Coca-Cola, you name it... even Facebook. All of these businesses have a specific niche and solve a problem.

To get started and begin doing the same, you're going first to need to choose the niche you want to focus on with your area. A niche is a specific segment of a market for any particular kind of product or service. Market niches are typically found around a subject matter or your section of an industry. For example, food would be a category, while vegan food would be a niche. A niche is more than a label. It also helps you define who your targeted audience is and what value you bring.

For restaurant owners and chefs, everyone isn't going to like your food, and that's okay. For foodies and influencers, everyone won't like your style of content, and that's okay. Therefore, don't waste time trying to convince or market to the people who don't like what you have to offer. Double down on what you're good at, and appreciate those that appreciate you. Take a look at some of the top chefs and celebrity cooks of the world today. If you pay attention, you will notice that they do not try to cater to everyone's preference. They have a distinct style or brand. They have their specific niche, and that's what they target.

Niche marketing is a significant key to brand success. It rings true for all aspects of food marketing and businesses too. Suppose you are a restaurant trying to find your social media niche. Look at what most of your audience and your fans have raved about when it comes to your food or business. Now, utilize that feedback and expand on it. You might find that what most of your audience's go-to, when they visit you, isn't what you are advertising on Instagram. If you already have an audience, check their tags and comments to see what they are really saying about you. Statements such as "Oh, you're a salmon is great, but we really loved your gumbo." or "They have good soup. But we really love their Red Beans & Rice!" are telling you what's most preferred. Listen to them. Feedback is vital for success in food.

Let's say maybe you are more of a Southern-style restaurant than an All-American restaurant. Or perhaps you are more of a personal chef than a caterer. I highly recommend that you have this figured out and define this upfront. Find your essential product, best service, or your top most requested product, and make sure you put it in the forefront. If you are a Chicken & Waffle's Spot but your customer's order and rate your Shrimp & Grits as the best, it's okay to share content about the dish. It doesn't hurt your brand or other products on the menu. If you don't describe it, you will miss out on people looking for what you have to offer, but because your profile doesn't mention it, they kept moving. Simply put, sell what they buy.

Specifically, if you're a chef or restaurant owner, you must control your social narrative. Take control of the wheel and steer your audience to what's in demand. The audience will come. You don't need to try to sell to the entire world. That is a huge mistake, and you will fail at the start. You must cater to your niche following.

While several Instagram blogs post random food content, you will find that the accounts with niche or consistent themes tend to do better. You will notice, even within what appears to be complete randomness, there is some similarity or some consistency within what they're posting. The most successful pages are targeting a particular demographic of people.

Research top influencers in your lane, figure out what they're doing, but also figure out what they're not doing. Figure out the content that they're not posting and the topics they're not talking about. What areas have they left uncovered? After you have figured all of this out, find what comes naturally to you out of everything you've discovered. That's what's going to make you stand out over everyone else. Also, this is what's going to help you with maintaining consistency. We will elaborate on why consistency is so important later.

Stay focused and dedicated to your brand. Don't get out of focus on what you're trying to accomplish. Don't look at other account's content and feel like you have to be like them. You can try different things, pick up new ideas, and even incorporate pieces of styles that you find to be cool. Your niche is who you are. Being you or your brand is the secret to a great niche. Don't try to duplicate what you see everyone doing. You can take technique and ideal, but your most valuable asset is you at the end of the day. Do your thing and put your spin on it. People love originality, especially on social media. Be different, be you. That's how you stand out, and the people in your niche find you on social media.

**TRY THIS!** (Instagram Insights)

Still not sure what's your social niche or most demanded of your products or brand? Try checking your Instagram insights to find out. Go to "Insights," then scroll down to "Content You Shared." From here, you can choose either "Posts" or "Stories" for details. Both of these will take you to the metrics page for the posts or stories you have shared in the last seven days to two years. This view is the "Select Metric" page. From here, you can begin to choose different metrics to see what works. Pick "Comments" to see what posts have gotten the most comments. You might be surprised to see the content that gets people to talk. Also, pick "Shares" to see what post people found interesting enough to share with others. You can also choose "Saves" to see what posts people are saving to come back to later.

All of this data gives you insights, hence the name, into what's working for you and your Instagram growth. Now that you've found what's working for your brand keep doing more of that. And watch your audience began to follow.

CHAPTER 3

# AUDIENCE

**D**efining your audience will be critical when looking to grow your Instagram page and build brand awareness. No matter if you are a chef, restaurant owner, food blogger, or influencer. You need to know who you're speaking to specifically before you can start building your brand's awareness. Now that you've identified the market niche you plan to support; you need to know who your audience is. So, in this chapter, we're going to define our audience profile.

Let me ask you a question, would you walk into a room full of strangers, start a conversation out loud, and hope someone randomly joins in with you? I didn't think so, and it probably sounds completely crazy when I put it that way. But that's how it looks when someone attempts to market to any and everyone on social media. Most social media accounts fail to attract followers because they don't understand their target audience or follower. So, who are they? What do they want? Where do they live? What are they interested in? Why should they follow you? All of these questions should be answered as you began to identify who is your target audience.

First, if you want to be recognized, specify who you're talking to when you post your content. If you're unsure of who your target audience is, start with the end in mind. What is your ultimate goal for posting this content? Who are you trying to influence or persuade? Or what message are you trying to get across? What does success look like for your brand and your business within this action?

Let's say you're a food influencer whose primary focus is to spread awareness of black representation disparities in your city's different spaces. Knowing and identifying your core audience will allow you to tailor your messaging to reach more like-minded individuals. This, in return, will start to build your brand's awareness and social growth as you pitch your content in a way that directly resonates with your audience.

Once you have recognized who you're content is speaking to, as you begin to directly address them, they will remember your brand and content. So let's define our audience. One of the most common practices and best approaches to doing this is creating a visual representation of your ideal customer or follower. This is what people refer to as a business personality, avatar, character, or customer profile. No matter what you call it, it still has the same effect. It's a visual representation of your business's personality. This would be the icon or the character like figure representing the particular people you're selling to or the group of people you feel is most interested in what you have to share. Developing or being aware of your social personality allows you to remain clear and aligned with your vision as you create content. Suppose you are posting something, and it doesn't seem like your business character. In most cases, if it's not a good fit for your brand, it probably won't connect well with your audience either. We will touch on good content creation in more detail in **Chapter 5: Content Strategy.**

Only by knowing your target audience is how you can begin to cater to your niche and speak to your core audience. For instance, let's take another look at the food influencer advocating for black cultural representation. They know that highlighting historical black figures will be appreciated because they are aware that the majority of their core audience is more than likely to be more socially conscious. Therefore, it is acceptable and well received by the audience.

Most of your content should cater to your audience by sharing content that adds value. This can be done in many ways, such as sharing menu information, cooking tips, and tools that support the customers of your business. Ideally, you want to find a need or problem and aid in solving it. That will draw in your ideal audience in any niche. If you're continually adding some form of value, your social is bound to gain attention.

After identifying your target audience, you need to know where to find them. There are a few different ways to do this. But here are a few that we found to be most effective. First, we recommend following the accounts with a similar interest or in the same category as your niche. By following the accounts of similar influencers, or leaders in the niche market you're currently in, you're able to keep your finger on the pulse of what's going on and contribute to the conversation. Knowing who the key players are in your niche also enables you to engage in the community where your ideal followers will be. Engaging in your niche community is vital for your growth. When you're not involved and engaged in your social community, others more than likely won't engage with you or deem your social account as creditable. And even if they do, the chances of them finding your account becomes slim.

The more people you follow in your peer group, the more likely they will follow you back. When they begin to notice, you are engaging with their content and similar pages that they also affiliate with or are known to be reputable, your social approval increases. In the social space, the more social approval you earn, the more likely the community of accounts will begin to accept and engage as they support your content.

Another way to find your audience is to follow hashtags relative to your niche. It seems pretty straightforward, but there are billions of hashtags to follow on Instagram. While a hashtag might be relevant to your account's niche, it also must be worth following. So you're going to want to pay attention to hashtags used by comparable accounts. Also, pay attention to the hashtags they're following.

As you begin to find different hashtags, you can also see who's following these hashtags. This only works if you're following the accounts that are following the hashtag. This is another benefit to following accounts with a similar niche as yours.

When you begin to follow hashtags or come across these hashtags, you will also see that your audience follows and uses them. Ideally, you're going to want to use hashtags that have a decent amount of followers. That way, you can come across more content and accounts relevant to what you're looking for and also engage in content similar to yours. By following the right mix of different hashtags key to your niche, you will be brought directly to where your audience resides.

You can do a quick hashtag search by looking up keywords relevant to your content. This can be accomplished by doing a Google search, searching hashtags within Instagram, and making a note of what other influencers are using.

For example, if you're a food blogger in DC, you should follow hashtags such as #DCfoodie, #DMVfood, and #DMV-foodiecrew. By following these hashtags, it will allow you to keep your finger on the pulse. And you will also be able to find new restaurants and content relative to your niche. Also, again, because you're following a few similar IG accounts.

You will pick up some of their hashtags and see them using and following the same hashtags or even new hashtags you may not be aware of. Don't consider this stealing. Utilize the hashtags that you see them using. It's more than likely that the post will pertain to the same content that you're posting. Artists are inspired by other artists all the time. So don't consider utilizing the hashtags that you see similar accounts using; as copying or stealing. In most cases, they're paying attention to what you're doing too.

You will have to do a little bit of profile research before buying into the hashtags accounts are using. When searching for hashtags, be sure to check them out first because people might use hashtags that are not relevant to their business. I don't recommend using all the hashtags you find an account using. Just because you were led to their page by one related hashtag doesn't mean all their hashtags are worth using. They could just be using anything relevant in the social media streets, which is a rookie attempt to gain traction or new followers. But don't worry too much about this. You will easily be able to weed out the accounts you should follow and engage with, versus the accounts that are not worth your time.

The third way we recommend you find your audience is by utilizing the Geotag feature on Instagram. On a typical day, there are 80 million photos shared on Instagram and 3.5 billion likes. With that in mind, most of the time, users who are posting photos at restaurants aren't aware of the trendy or best hashtags to use. Let's face it, most of the time, we don't even know if a restaurant has an Instagram account or where to go about finding it. Typically, food or the daily special is the first thing restaurants are advertising. So when customers post photo's of their food, assuming they use the restaurant's location. Everyone who supports or goes to the restaurant can find the picture under the restaurant's Geotag. If they post the photo while they're in the place, Instagram will even suggest it under the location. So how does this benefit you? Well, you can find an audience of potential customers, foodies, and content that wasn't tagged with the account or hashtags. This is an Instagram influencer trick most people are completely unaware of.

There are many untapped opportunities that people forget to take advantage of by not utilizing the geolocation search. When you run across any event, or a restaurant, or a location that has anything going on pertaining to your niche, you should do a search on Instagram. You might be surprised at how quickly you will find several restaurants, foodies, and pockets of communities that support them.

Finally, an excellent way to find your audience and gain new followers is to like the likers. This is actually a secret technique that helps customers find you and increases your Instagram following and brand awareness.

So what is liking the likers? Well, after you have identified accounts that are similar or in the same niche as your account, go to their profile and look at their posts. Then go into the like section of some of their post. For each of these posts, look at the accounts that are liking their content. Now go into the "likers" profiles and like some of their content.

Profiles that are liking similar accounts' content and engaging in their post will probably find your content interesting too. You don't have to become a spammer when doing this. Casually search and like the likers content that's relevant to your brand. Comment and engage with authentic responses. Liking two to three of their recent post will get their attention. Out of curiosity, most users will check out your profile to see who's liking their content after they notice that you have liked and engaged in some of their posts. This single strategy will increase your following and allow you to find your customers exponentially. This will also increase your following and your influence on those accounts that are interested.

I highly recommend that you don't do an auto-copy and paste approach when commenting and messaging directly to these accounts because it can come off spammy. Please don't; you will need to truly engage in your niche and community. Liking three, five at the most, of their most recent posts and leaving a comment relevant to what they posted is key for growth. This is especially true for reaching out to influencers and much larger accounts. Messages are best received when it's authentically tailored and based on our reaction to the content versus something that can be seen as a bot. Maintain awareness of the top influencer's accounts, and stay on the lookout for new hashtags and search the locations where the action might be for your niche. These approaches will not only work for any Instagram accounts that are food-related, but they will work for all Instagram accounts. In a world full of bots, authentic engagement will always win their attention before the other.

## CHAPTER 4

# PROPER PROFILE

They say a first impression is a lasting impression. However, when it pertains to Instagram, a first impression is a chance to gain a new follower. Therefore you must make sure your profile can attract new followers. Ideally, when someone stumbles on to your Instagram page, you want your profile set up to gain their interest enough that they want to follow you. The initial thing that everyone will see when they land on your Instagram profile page is a profile picture, bio, and any links that you have listed. Let's review the aspects of a catchy profile image, components of the name, biography, and links.

### Profile Picture

To start, let's look at the profile image. Your profile image is going to depend on the type of business you have. Let's say you are a restaurant owner, and you want to have your restaurant's marquee or logo as your profile picture. You would need to make sure the logo is clear and appealing to the eye. People should be able to see it, identify with it, and know who you are at first sight. For example, if you were to look at McDonald's Instagram page, you will see their golden arches logo. It's their business logo, and the golden arches are always used in their marketing. It's their branding, and people think of the company at the sight of the logo. Using it as a profile logo creates a familiarity that automatically helps people identify with the business profile. If you're a chef, you may have a logo or image you use for marketing. We recommend that this image is a high-resolution photo of yourself, your business logo, or an avatar that looks like you.

Ensure that you choose a profile picture relevant to your niche and what your Instagram account is about. One of the mistakes most accounts make is that they will use a picture of something unrelated to their content as their profile picture. If you are a chef or caterer, using an image of you standing next to a plane or sitting on the beach as your profile picture doesn't help your branding. Create masterpieces of food, or you in a chef coat or inaction would work better to promote your brand's awareness. Even if you don't use a picture of yourself or your restaurant location, using a distinct logo or business visual will serve your social brand awareness well.

Also, a picture of food as your profile image won't look as appealing in the 110 X 110 pixels display Instagram gives you. However, if your logo or branding has your name and food within it, that will work as well. Whichever you do, you want to make sure that the colors are attractive and the profile picture is clear. You are going to want to use a high-resolution profile picture. Image clarity is crucial. Images that look distorted or of low quality speaks of your brand and the quality level you represent. If you're a chef or influencer, using a high-quality profile picture is a necessity.

Your profile picture should relate to your business or message. So if you are a food blogger, make sure that your profile picture has some visuals related to your blogging or content.

Some of the best influencers and food bloggers, you will typically see the representation of their brand in their profile picture. They also might be holding some food or have some indication of what they do. For example, in an influencer's profile picture, they might have a shirt with either their name, a business, or a phrase related to what they do. Another tip is if you're selling merch along with your blog, you can also wear some of the merch in your profile picture. This works well, especially when the shirt or merch represents your brand and targets your audience or community. Whatever you do, getting the profile picture right is highly important. You want people to click on your profile picture when they come across your content on the Explorer page or down their feed. Your profile picture will play a big part in attracting your targeted audience to click on your profile to look into the rest of your information and content.

It might sound silly, but people will judge your food's taste and your business by the quality of your photos. We will go more into content creation in greater detail later on. For now, if you don't have a good profile picture, you need to get a photographer or someone with a good camera phone to take your photo or have an image for your business created.

## Your IG Name

A great Instagram username will help you get found organically. You're going to want to be very careful about the Instagram username you decide to use. Suppose you're a restaurant owner who already established a name outside of Instagram. In that case, you're going to want to find that name for your Instagram username. The best approach is always to find the exact or closest username to your restaurant name as possible. Having the same name username as your business name will help customers or supporters become aware of your restaurant and find you on Instagram.

The first thing people will typically search for when looking for your restaurant is the business name. The same thing also applies to chefs and caterers. If you are "Chef XYZ," you will want to have the username "Chef XYZ" on Instagram or something close to it. Your username will become more important to your success as you continue to brand and market yourself.

When soliciting business, people may not remember that your Instagram username is @Supernovaeats808. Especially if your actual chef's name is Chef Clarissa Monroe, make sure that people can find you by using the same name you're marketing yourself. Also, you want to avoid using periods, underscores, and numbers. On Instagram, the username is limited to 30 characters, and you're only allowed to use letters, numbers, periods, and underscores. You are also not allowed to include symbols, emojis, or other punctuation marks as a part of your username. Choosing a username different from your brand name and using too many underscores, numbers or periods will be confusing and increase the difficulty for others to find you.

Aside from your Instagram Username, there is also an opportunity to capitalize on the Instagram Profile Name. The profile name is the name that appears in bold under your profile picture. Let's say your actual chef name is Chef Dev, but it was unavailable for your username, so you used your catering company name "FlavorFavors901". The profile name section is the perfect opportunity to list your name as Chef Dev.

It's also important to use a profile name that's easily recognizable and distinguished to define what you do or who you are. The same rules apply to the profile name as it does to the username. So you want to make sure to load up your Instagram bio name with as many keywords as possible. Just make sure that you are using the important keywords related to your niche to gain the right type of traffic.

So here's a secret technique that most people aren't aware of with the profile name. Because of your ability to add up to 30 characters, you have the opportunity to add more searchable keywords to the end or beginning of your profile name. You can add keywords or short descriptors that will help boost your search traffic and or some form of social status. Let's say these keywords probably didn't make sense for your username, or you wish you could have included them. To help distinguish yourself, add niche-specific trendy words with your name. Check some of our examples of two to three buzzwords in your niche after your profile name.

**Example:**

Joes Cafe | Best Coffee Dallas

Chef XYZ | Celebrity Chef

Keyal Eats African Foodie

Black Foodie Finder App

Remember that Instagram is searchable through Google and other search engines as well. So it's best to make sure that you list your name or brand the same way it's used when conducting business or how you prefer for people to find you. For example, if you're a restaurant owner, putting the word "restaurant" behind the business name makes it much easier for people looking for a restaurant or your business's name in a crowded social space. It also helps people who stumble onto your profile quickly identify who you are and what type of service you have to offer.

It's not required that you list your name exactly as you have, but this helps someone who is searching for your IG page. Especially if you go by multiple names, alternative names, or you weren't able to get a user name that was the same or close to your actual name. Your username and profile name are two of the most critical components to having success on Instagram. The reason being is because they are the only two keyword sections that are searchable pieces of information on your profile. So it's going to be important that the naming convention you use for your Instagram account aligns with the name you use on other social media accounts. You want to make yourself easy to find. Also, keep in mind your website, business cards, and anything you may incorporate or trademark will probably use or have the same or similar name. The more places you can consistently use your name, the more your brand recognition and awareness grows. Also, by using a consistent naming convention, you are more likely to increase the traffic that comes across your profile because you are search-friendly.

So what if you're an influencer or food blogger and you don't have a name yet? How do you find your name for your Instagram account? Well, I would recommend using terms that have your niche within it. Let's look at us, for example, "Black Foodie Finder." We highlight black chefs, restaurants, and foodies, making it easier for supporters to find them. Therefore, if anyone is searching for "black food," "black foodies," or "Find Black food," we will more than likely pop up as a popular search. Using simple terms also helps drive search traffic and visibility. As you're finding the right name, look at what's already in use in your industry.

Finding the right name helps us stand out and distinguish ourselves amongst other profiles in a crowded field. It also lets people know who you are at first sight. If somebody who's African American and considers themselves a foodie was to see the profile name, "Black Foodie Finder," when they see the word "Foodie," it will be an easy follow for them. In most cases, because of the titling, a clear connection is already established for them.

You don't want to use the same name as someone else, and sometimes it is hard not to come close to similar titles. However, it doesn't hurt to use the most popular terms in your niche. This method is especially true when you're using general universal terms, such as black & food. Several Instagram accounts use the terms black and food in some combination, and that's completely okay. Nothing is wrong with a slight similarity. Some would even recommend doing it to catch more traffic. Besides, it's your style and content that will make you stand out from the rest. Just make sure that you're original in whatever you decide to do. And remember, your Instagram name also represents your brand and what you do. So make a statement.

## Bio Section Upgrade

**Bio Section:** Once people land on your Instagram profile, the next thing they're going to see besides your profile image is the bio section. Many Instagrammers miss the step of creating a good bio for their profile that will spark interest. The perfect Instagram bio should have a story, make a statement, stand out, and identify its value.

Chefs often get this one wrong by mentioning things that have nothing to do with their Instagram page or business. The bio section is a golden opportunity to introduce your brand to newcomers and give those already following your profile more details. Maximize on the chance and also give them a few things that they may not have been aware of that are related to your business. The profile picture is great for being seen, but it's the bio section that seals the deal for most of your soon to be followers.

Your bio section is where you capture your audience into determining if they're going to follow your account or not. When new accounts land on your profile, they may want to know who they're following and what they're getting themselves into. If your bio doesn't appeal to people who come across your profile, more than likely, they won't even scroll through your content. Most people don't like to follow an account without knowing what to expect from them. The bio allows you to summarize your niche in a short statement and call out what makes you stand out from the rest. Minimally, it would be best if you defined three things in your bio: who you are, what you do, and where to find what to do. If you get those three things right and concise, you will see more growth in your Instagram page in combination with good content. So this is your chance to make a first impression to gain a new follower.

## Who are you?

This isn't just the name of your restaurant or the chef name that you go by? Or what they call you in your line of business? Or what's the name of your food blog? It's a simple question that countless Instagram accounts get wrong.

First, let's define who you are. The answer to this question isn't just your restaurant's name, the chef name you go by, or what they call you in your line of business. Nor is it the name of your food blog. It's a simple question that countless Instagram accounts get wrong. So, who are you?

There's more to it than a title. You're defining who you are considered to be in your niche. For example, let's look at the IG account of The Turkey Leg Hut (@turkeyleghut). If you were to look at their profile, their username is their business's name, making it easy to find. Their profile name tells you the full business name "The Turkey Leg Hut & Company," which gives you another way to search for them by their business name. And within their bio, the first line tells you who they are. "We are The Originators of The World Famous Stuffed Turkey Legs!". That's telling you who they are in the food space. Making it known to followers who you are should be summed up in a couple of words or a one-line sentence. It doesn't need to be a long and drawn out story. Besides, Instagram only gives you a 150 bio character limit. You don't want your bio to be too busy or too much to read and make sense of. It needs to be very short, concise, and to the point that it tells people who you are.

So let's define how you answer this question. Look at the personality, core beliefs, and values of your brand. What do you consider to be most important to your brand? What are you known for? What do people ask of you the most?

Let's say you have a wing spot in Atlanta, Georgia. And of all of the wing sauces that you have to offer, your most popular sauce is your *hot lemon pepper wings* that you originated. Identifying this in the opening statement of who you are is a perfect start to your bio statement. See the examples below.

## Example

"Famous East ATL wing spot known for our signature Hot Lemon Pepper Wings."

"Vegan Cafe, 100% plantbased."

"Always Hungry! Traveling Food Blogger"

"NOLA Private Chef"

Answering the question of who you are, gives you a chance to let people know about you or your business. If you don't know where to start answering the question of "Who you are?" ask yourself, what are you known for? What is your impact? Or what role do you fill in your niche? If you don't have a product, then look at what skills you have to offer. What are you good at? Maybe there is something that you're passionate about that drives you. If you're a food blogger or influencer, what is it that you're most passionate about? What is the topic or area of interest that you share throughout social media?

Another tip for approaching this task is finding a keyword that is actively used in your niche or profile and then building your story around it. By including keywords that pertain to your niche or profile, you increase the chances of those with the same interest follows you.

Answering these questions will also help you find the next part of the bio section. "What do you do?". After you've identified who you are in your bio, you should let people know what it is that you do. The statement of "Who are you?" actually builds up, supports, and, in some cases, includes the answer to the question "What do you do?".

When you answer the question, "what do you do?" you're actually answering the question, "How can you help them." You want to make a point of letting people know how you can assist them, what you can give them, and what you can do for them. Make your statement appealing; for example, "Soul food restaurant" doesn't sound as attractive as "Serving Upscale Creole Southern Comfort Food." Besides telling them about your food or service, there's also an opportunity to let them know your worth. Many Instagrammers will use this moment as an opportunity to insert some form of social proof. Social proof is a statement where you let others know of any awards, accolades, or accomplishments that highlight what makes you stand out from the crowd. Make sure that this statement ties back into who you are. Social proof statements should be short, direct, and concise, letting people understand your niche and what role you fill in the market.

An example of this would be mentioning something like "Yelp voted #1 Soul Food Restaurant 2020" or "Featured in Essence Eats." These are statements that add value by flexing some of your social proof and accolades. Both will still provide insight into what you can or have to offer them.

To find your "what do you do" statement, ask yourself, "What job do you get done?" or "What do task do you seek to accomplish from your social presents?". You want to make this attractive, catchy, and exciting. So, for example, let's look at The Turkey Leg Hut again. Here's their "What we do" statement: "We offer a unique dining experience that our customers can't get enough of!"

Suppose we begin to dissect this statement. We can quickly figure out that The Turkey Leg Hut is a dining restaurant. They have a unique niche that they fill, which the sentence before this one tells us that its turkey legs. And lastly, their customers are acclaimed to enjoy their food, which means they are doing something right. That tells me enough to want to find out more about this restaurant. You want to find the selling point or bragging line about what you have to offer through a short story or a couple of lines. But remember not to overcrowd your bio. A messy, crowded bio section can also be a turnoff to people.

It may also be helpful for restaurant owners to add their hours of operation and where to find their full menu. You also may want to add useful tidbits of information that will help potential customers find what they need and save you time. Pay attention to frequently asked questions that customers are calling or emailing you about. If it's short, here's a chance to put it in the bio. If it's detailed, such as menu items, you can tell them where to locate it. This will free you and your team up from taking calls that pull you away from doing other important things.

There's also the opportunity to utilize hashtags in your bio. If you have a branded hashtag, dropping it in your bio will take your viewers to content using your hashtag. When you have a specific hashtag that you use for your business, it also allows you to find reviews and content others post related to your brand. It's an excellent opportunity to use it in your bio because it helps people quickly know that it's your hashtag. This also makes it simple for people to find your post and create new leads as people discover your hashtag and follow it.

## Examples for "What You Do" statement

The Sprinkle Factory (@the_sprinkle_Factory) - *Cookbook Author, Food Content Creator, Professional Chef*

Ash Cash Exantus (@iamashcash) - *One of America's Leading Financial Educators*

Black Restaurant Week (@blackrestaurantweek) - *Black Restaurant Week is a movement celebrating Pan-African cuisine.*

Finally, your bio should include where you are located or where to find what you do. If you are in the business of providing, this is going to be crucial for you. Restaurant owners, chefs, and caterers need to have their location or where they operate so potential customers can find them. Countless restaurants and people in the food industry miss this step when updating their profiles. You don't want someone who comes to your IG page and see that you have all of this delicious food, but they don't know where to find it. The vast majority of people are not going to go through the trouble of trying to direct message(DM) you or email you for your food. So it's going to be very important that you make it as simple as possible to find where your restaurant is located. Even if you don't have a brick-and-mortar location, you should mention the general area you serve and cater to.

I can't tell you how many restaurants, chefs, and catering companies' Instagram profile I come across with no location or address. And there's absolutely no way to figure out where their business is located except for direct messaging them. Leaving off your location is a huge mistake. You miss out on countless local opportunities and potential customers who may be right in your city that would not know you're available.

If you are not a chef, or you don't serve food. Maybe you're a food blogger or your influencer? Do you have a website? Do you have a landing page? Do you have a product that you're selling? If you have any of these, let them know about it here.

For foodies, food blogs, and influencers. While your physical location isn't as important, where to find your work will be necessary. Keep in mind that you don't own Instagram.

You may want to direct followers to your blog site, website, YouTube channel, or any other source where you have a collection of your work. For example, you may want to direct followers to a link to capture their email so you can stay in contact with them. This is where you want to list your website or somewhere that they can get directly to you without Instagram.

This leads us to our final recommendation for a highly effective Instagram bio, your call to action. A call-to-action (CTA) is a marketing term for any statement that directly prompts someone to respond immediately or take action based on your directions. For reference, call-to-action is also called a CTA for short. A call to action is a great way to direct leads and prospects to your website or links in your bio. There's also an opportunity to use a CTA to share info with follows who may not be aware of or aren't already taking action on something you have previously offered in a post. As you can see, there's an endless amount of opportunities you can capitalize on by using a good CTA in your bio.

A call-to-action can be in the form of a story, but we recommend that you keep it short and concise for the bio. Reminder, we don't have a lot of space here. We want to make sure we can maximize the opportunity to capture someone's attention when landing on our page. We can lose people if it's too wordy.

Now, the real secret to a good call-to-action is that you want to make sure it's a strong one that convinced people to act as soon a possible. You may find that many Instagram profiles have a call to action, so it's not enough to have a simple statement such as, "follow me!". You want to make sure that you have a strong and convincing call to action that invokes people to move. To best accomplish this, you want to create some form of urgency or extreme value.

So an example of a call to action would look like "Follow us for more food content," "Tag us for shares," or "Download

Our Free Recipe Book." These would be examples of calls to action because they direct people to act upon something you want them to do.

When a good call-to-action accompanies a sound bio section, the viewer will feel compelled to move on to the offer presented to them. Remember, they will act on it based on everything they have seen so far from your Instagram page.

A call to action does not always need to sell. Sometimes, you just need to get the customer a little bit more intimate with your business. We will give you more examples of CTA's later as we review **Chapter 5: Content Strategy**.

Remember, the bio is the chance to captivate your audience by letting them know who you are and what you do in your niche. There are billions of restaurants, chefs, and food bloggers. However, our individuality makes us who we are, regardless of the niche or business space that we operate in.

You need to make sure that your IG bio is appealing and concise. You should be super clear about who you are targeting, and your sure that your message translates to the audience you plan to attract. You are not only trying to target your niche audience with your bio statement. You also want to convert anyone who stumbles upon your Instagram account and wants to know what you do or what you have that will benefit them.

The bio is where you want to give them everything they need to know to decide if they're going to follow you or not. This is your chance to express what makes you different from everyone else. If you nail it in the bio, more than likely, you're going to be able to grab the attention of newcomers to convert them into followers, supporters or engage in your content.

By applying the tips listed in this chapter, you'll begin to gain followers and increase engagement when you have created a magnet Instagram profile. Most importantly, establish brand awareness that puts you in a position of authority and helps you establish an instant brand presence in your niche.

## CHAPTER 5

# CONTENT STRATEGY

One of the most significant issues that people face is not being aware of how their Instagram content may affect their audience's engagement. People tend to pay more attention to what they find attractive and interesting. Therefore, as you know, the content that you use will be extremely important to your success, especially for restaurants and chefs. When it comes to creating good content, there's a multitude of different strategies and angles that you can take. However, we will cover some of the best practices and methods that are known to work in the food industry on Instagram.

First, let's cover the dynamics of creating a post. There are two ways to create content, either making original content or reposting others' content. Original content is when you release any form of media that has never been released to the public before. For those in the business of selling food, the original content will play a crucial role in your content strategy. Advertising your food will have to be original content unless you only rely on your customers' posting content. We recommend you figure out a system for content creation early because it will affect how often you post and your ability to keep your audience engaged.

Most restaurant owners and chefs will create original content because they must show their work and products to their potential customers. So with that being said, it's going to be extremely vital that you're able to take great photos of your food. So let's look at what makes a great food photo.

First, for restaurants, while getting a professional photographer, or a high-class cameraman, to take your photos is great for significant photo shoots. However, when it comes to social media and creating new content daily, we recommend using your phone. We've noticed that pictures directly from the phone tend to convert better and gain more traction than very high-quality professional photos.

Surprisingly, we've found that the phones that are now available today, they're almost equivalent to very high-quality photo cameras. If you were to compare the Apple iPhone 12 Pro to a high-quality Nikon DSLR camera, you would find that the iPhone can achieve similar professional photos. Not to mention that a quality Nikon DSLR typically costs around $4,000 without lens attachments, while the iPhone cost around $1,000. That makes using your phone the preferred choice for many Instagram food photographers.

We recommend that you are using a phone that is up to date with the latest technology. For your IG content strategy, photos and videos have to be of high-resolution quality. Your pictures need to be high resolution and clear because it speaks of your brand's quality, and that's what will connect the most with viewers. Low quality and blurry or pixel distorted images don't do well or receive nearly the same amount of attention as a good quality image.

And so, to take a good food photo, one of the essential elements is lighting. There are two types of lighting that you can use, which are artificial lighting and natural lighting. We've found that natural lighting tends to work best for food photos. However, if you do need to use artificial lighting, make sure that it's well lit. Natural lighting from the sun always works well for food photos. You may find that sitting a plate of food next to a window, or even going outside of the restaurant for an outdoor photoshoot, will highlight the food attributes when taking pictures. For natural lighting, this also applies to video content. We do not recommend taking food photos in low or dim-lit areas. What tends to happen is the food tends to look dull, and the camera isn't able to pick up the highlights of the food needed to make the image look more appealing.

If you're shooting in the dark, make sure that you use some form of lighting or spotlighting to catch the food. What tends to happen with food and dark and dim pictures is that the food comes out looking dull and blurry. In such darkness, the camera may not be able to autofocus. Food should have a vibrant light and color to it. Most of the time, using the right lighting can make the food pop out.

Also, when using your camera, we do not recommend zooming in on the food. If you need to get an up-close shot, bring the phone closer. Zooming in to take the photo will affect the resolution and the quality of the pictures. Pictures of food that's zoomed in and blew up to appear closer tend not to look that well.

When shooting photos outside, make sure that your food isn't overexposed to direct sunlight. While you want natural light, you should shoot on a day where the clouds are out just a little bit or doing hours of the day that there isn't too much light directly from the sunlight. The morning is typically the best time of day for outside shots. Too much sunlight over-exposes the image; losing detail is due to harsh lighting. If you take photos in high sunlight areas of high sunlight, we recommend turning on your HDR option on your phone to balance the lighting.

In most cases, if your camera has the HDR, high dynamic range option, we recommend using it. You can toggle back and forth to see the difference, but HDR will do your photos justice in most cases. When you're doing a food photoshoot, we recommend taking multiple pictures from multiple angles and trying some overheads. The more shots you're able to get, the more photos you can pick and utilize later for content batching. Also, because you've taken pictures from so many different angles and views, your media won't become stale to your viewers when you post it.

Batching is creating multiple posts or content at one time and then scheduling them for later. For restaurant owners or chefs with a busy schedule, batching your Instagram content will save you time and reduce stress. Serving, cooking, and dealing with customers is a full-time job in itself. To effectively grow your Instagram following, you will need quality content. Assuming the majority of your Instagram post are going to be original content. In that case, you need to find a process that allows you to produce content and save time consistently.

Imagine yourself creating a new post on Instagram each day. You have to come up with an idea, picture, and caption. If you didn't have any fresh food photos on your phone, you would be trying to take one in the midst of your busy day. Let's not forget that this should be a quality photo or video to represent your brand. It sounds time-consuming, especially when you're doing this multiple times a day or week.

This is why you should schedule some time so you can take a bunch of different pictures and videos of your food from multiple angles. Then you need to plan out your Instagram feed. This will require you to look at your calendar and lay-out what your next few posts will be like and be about. You can batch content for a week or month; it's entirely up to you. Last, we recommend you go through the process of actually creating these posts without posting them to your feed. Instead of posting them, save the content with everything set up, so all you need to do is post when you're ready. There are several apps that can make this process easier.

## APPS for Batching

Preview

Later

Buffer

Hootsuite

We personally use the Preview app. We use it more for data than batching but found it to work well with batching content. As you are getting multiple batching shots, think about different ways you can utilize and switch up the media form. For example, getting various photos from different angles, so it doesn't look like it's the same plate.

You can also piece together video content. Extra pieces of footage and different forms of media will help you later with having more content to use. When shooting a food video, if you're not talking about the food or given direct commentary, we recommend that you use some music in the background. Marketing researchers find that sound can automatically direct our visual attention and even influence us to make purchases. Our studies have shown that food videos with no sound tend to get fewer likes and engagement versus food videos with some type of music in the background. Several options are available for background music and overlay music that you can utilize from different websites. Story Blocks is a website that we use for copyright-free background music.

If you created an influencer or personal brand, it's okay to be a little bit looser in your post. Nevertheless, you need to be consistent and make sure that you are posting relevant content daily. Aside from that, this brings us to our next point. You want to be able to have and utilize various media types of content that you're posting.

Mixing up your use of the media form in the type of posts and content you're pushing out will also help your engagement and growth. For example, with photos, sometimes you want to utilize Instagram carousels. Within your carousel, a content strategy that we recommend is using a few multiple angles of the food that you're posting. This is because everyone doesn't have the same taste and preference, even when it comes to images. There is going to be someone who prefers looking at the food a little bit closer in detail. There's going to be others that want to get a far back plated shot, just enough to see some of the scenery. Then some love the overhead view. So you want to try to utilize multiple angles within your post's carousel. Suppose someone was to scroll past a picture in your carousel without liking it. In that case, Instagram will then show them some of the other photos in your carousel down their timeline. These are a few reasons carousels perform better than single-shot posts.

Also, we found that utilizing videos mixed in with photos tend to work really well for engagement. While images are great for capturing that perfect shot, a video works well for grabbing attention. The average IG user scrolls down 300 feet of social media content per day, and they're usually scrolling pretty quickly. When a video comes across their feed, most people will stop for a second to see what's going on. This is your moment to "reel" them in. If your content is good, the viewer will stay engaged.

In addition to that, videos seem to connect because people can see the food in live-action throughout the video post. For a video post of food, you also want to move around a food a little bit to give people a better view of it.

Check out some of the other people posting food and take notice of the different camera motions they're using. There are a lot of different techniques, such as slow-motion zooming into the meal, the swaying back and forth boat rocking, and the stop-n-go video techniques. Of course, there will be different preferences and opinions on which looks better, but that's for you and your audience to decide. We found that sometimes swaying videos make people feel seasick, but many people love those too. So mix it up a little bit and test what works for your audience. Whatever you decide to do, keep creating and trying new techniques as a part of your original content.

Instagram gives you the option to post photos, videos, reels, and stories. We recommend utilizing all of these options when it comes to pushing out your content. Post variety is going to help your social footprint and brand awareness spread over Instagram.

## Repurposing & Reposting

Reposting is the act of posting something again. You can re-purpose anything; your content or the content of others. If it's was previously posted and you post it also, consider it as a repost.

To keep up with consistently providing useful content is not as easy as it seems. That's where repurposing or curating content offers a helping hand. Repurpose content from others who have similar related content. Just make sure the post you curate or repurpose is relevant to your audience. The best part about reposting is that it's a completely ethical marketing practice. Most don't consider it plagiarism, as long as you give credit. Either tag or mention the original poster is how most people give credit; we do both.

While original content can be your brand's competitive advantage, you should also consider utilizing others' content. Reposting content can also have a ton of advantages. For now, let's focus on how this benefits your content strategy. Reposting is the act of posting something again; you can repurpose anything, your content, or the content of others. If someone posted it before you, and you post it after, consider it as a repost.

Reposting the content of others allows you to benefit from the work of others. For most people on Instagram, reposting content is their only way of creating media. For chefs and restaurant owners, using content from your customers, supporters, or just other profiles in general, gives you the benefit and advantage of saving time and energy as well as social proof.

Most chefs and restaurant owners repost their customers' and supporters' content about them because it gives them the advantage of having handpicked reviews to highlight their work. Sharing their content allows other followers to see that people are genuinely purchasing or enjoying the services you bring.

Another reason reposting is suitable for restaurants, chefs, and caterers is because it saves them a lot of time. If you're creating dishes, running a business, or serving customers, your time is probably limited. So it's helpful when people decide to take great pictures of your creations or you and then post them. If they tag you, these are additional pictures that you didn't have to take, and you now have the option to utilized them to showcase your talents. Food bloggers and influencers tend to utilize reposting more heavily. Resharing content allows them the chance to take advantage of others' work and appear in spaces that they may not be able to get to physically. No matter who you are, part of your content strategy should be built around staying consistent.

When reposting content, we recommend that you make sure that you do a quality control check before posting. Ensure that the content you're repurposing meets or comes close to the same standards as the content you already have.

Lastly, when it pertains to a content strategy, utilizing reposted content allows you to cherry-pick the content that best fits your feed and audience demographic. Instead of making the content that matches your feed, the entire world of Instagram is at your fingertips to use whatever content works best for your audience.

## Good Content - The 4 C's

So you might be wondering, overall, what makes a good post? And what's considered a good content strategy. We have created what we like to call "The four C's." The four C's consist of clarity, consistency, caption, and call to action. These are the four ingredients we recommend when creating a piece of content.

**Clarity:** Clarity is going to be vital as it pertains to quality and creating content. Ideally, you would want your content to come across crisp and clear because it represents quality. Your content should be valuable and captivating, as well as clearly articulating what you're trying to convey in each post. From the visual aspect, it will be extremely important for anyone in the food industry to make sure that their pictures are of high or excellent quality. If you are a restaurant owner, and you're just establishing your brand. It's going to be vital that you set a standard of quality inside your restaurant and outside with your marketing.

Suppose the content that you are posting does not come across as visually appealing to the eyes. In that case, you will not draw in as many followers as those who do.

When the content you create does not have a great visual representation, viewers will begin to value your brand at the level of the content they see. That may not seem like a big thing, but people buy with their eyes when it comes to food on social media.

They will judge your food quality by what you have visually shown them first before they decide to book your private catering services or walk into your restaurant. So make sure that you use high-resolution photos and videos with captivating content when you are pushing your brand on Instagram. Typically, we find that restaurants that use low-quality imagery lose engagement and see minimum traffic. Also, they are typically seen as small town mom & pop restaurants. If you are an established restaurant or building a restaurant brand, your marketing will be key.

You don't have to spend a lot of cash to create quality content consistently. There are different tools available, such as Canva, for your content and marketing creation. It doesn't take a lot, but you do have to be intentional about representing yourself.

**Consistency:** When we're looking at content strategy, regularly showing up on Instagram is important. But it isn't just about consistently posting on a daily basis. It's also about being consistent with the type of content that you're posting. People are showing up and following you, expecting a certain kind of content. So you have to be consistent with what you're providing. Suppose you're posting food pictures and articles, and you decide to switch your content to dance videos. The chances are that most people will not like it or engage in this content. They didn't follow you for dance videos. They chose to follow you for food content. Making drastic switches to the type of content you're posting can hurt your engagement and confuse your audience. When your followers see content and don't like it or engage with it, that lowers your engagement percentage. Because fewer people are noticing the content, fewer people are noticing you, and that stagnates your growth on Instagram. It's important to continue to show up with the content that falls into the category of what your followers are expecting.

See our "bad content switch up" example of the <ins>dance video</ins> we posted. (NOTE: I viewers didn't like this content with we first posted it.)

You can post different content, but don't stray away from your core. Ever notice restaurant accounts that post things far outside of food? It typically doesn't do so well. You can step out of the box from time to time but focusing on your niche is where you will see the quickest result in growth. Even when you're making content, the quality of your present content also needs to be consistent. Suppose you're showing high-resolution videos and pictures. You don't want to switch to granular or low-quality content.

In most cases, you will not receive the same engagement as your other content making drastic switches. Remember, the goal is rapid growth on Instagram. And you do it by continuing to show up, providing the content that your know your followers are expecting.

**Caption:** One of the most forgotten components of a good posting content strategy is your caption. Having a good caption will help Instagram users scroll and engage in your content. Part of your growth and content strategy is that you want users to interact with your content for more extended periods.

Instagram tracks how long a user watches and engages in your content. The typical user swipes past posts within less than a second. So when you are creating text, you need to make it captivating enough to engage the users, so they follow through to view more.

Instagram also places value on how long someone views your post. The algorithms favor content that's viewed for more extended periods because it signals to them that viewers are enjoying your content and it's worth sharing with others. Content such as this is what you may find on the explore page.

To effectively draw in our audience, we need to be aware of who our audience is and/or what they want. Who we're speaking to can change depending on the piece of content your sharing. Knowing what your audience needs and what you are trying to convey to them will be important, and it also should provide some value to the viewer. For example, a chef showing their audience how to create a dish may inform your audience of the ingredients or additional tips in the caption.

As you're creating a caption, you want to make sure it meshes well with the media you have above it. Also, depending on the picture or video you are posting, if you didn't have the opportunity to explain everything in the content, you could utilize the caption to give more details for anything that wasn't included in the video. Maybe it's posting a lunch special or something that you're serving for a particular day. Your audience wouldn't be aware of this without more details. So in your caption, this could be the opportunity to let them know about these details that weren't in the media.

Questions, stories, call-to-actions, help information, entertaining, or uplifting, as you can see, there are many options and opportunities when creating a caption. Just remember that the first 125 characters of your caption will only show until the viewer clicks the option "more" on your post. So with this being said, you want to ensure that your caption is attention-grabbing, especially within the first 125 characters. An excellent approach to creating a strong lead and for your caption would be to ask a question. You can start by asking your audience something that will make them want to engage and answer back. Another right approach is to lead in with a shock value statement or a polarizing statement. Your audience will be so caught off guard by your statement that they will almost feel impelled to click through to find out what else you're about to say behind your statement.

There isn't a shortcut for authentic engagement. However, using solid captions will drive measurable interactions from your audience. Captions are tricky, and there are many ways to approach them. No matter what you do. No matter which one of the approaches you decide to use, the best premises for a caption will be to either entertain, inspire or inform your audience.

**Call-to-action (CTA):** As we've mentioned before, a call to action is direct or specific instructions to your followers to act or do as you advise. Why is this so important? Because your call-to-action is what's going to help you grow your platform and convert followers into customers. A call-to-action enables you to bring new customers into your restaurant, book new clients, gain new followers, and sell products or services you may provide. This is how you can capitalize on your content. Using a call-to-action, points out directly what you need your audience to do.

It's not enough to just post the content you have and hope that your followers and audience know what product or service you are providing. It's also not going to be enough just to display your services and expect people to take advantage of your offer. You have to let them know what you want them to do.

A call-to-action will look something like a restaurant owner saying, "Come in and try our new barbecue ribs." In the caption of the picture of some smoked barbecue glazed ribs. They could have posted this without a call-to-action, but would they really want to leave it up to the viewer to figure out. And they may even have said these are new ribs on the menu, but to actually tell your audience to come in and try it can be the difference that makes some people actually do it.

Combine these four components to your content: Clarity, Consistency, Caption, and a Call-to-action. Plus, including the tips of focusing on quality visuals, you will be surprised to see how well even your most simple post performs.

## CHAPTER 6

# GROWTH STRATEGY

Now that we've covered the foundational pieces that will set your Instagram up for success, less focus on your Instagram account's intentional growth.

## Grow
### <u>Consistency</u>

The first thing you're going to need to focus on is consistency. That means you need to be consistent in your posting frequency and the type of content your posting. You must show up regularly and continually producing a similar level of content to grow on Instagram. For Chefs & Restaurant owners, you need to post more frequently on a day-to-day basis.

It doesn't matter if you're a restaurant owner, an influencer, chef, or blogger; your consistency will play a huge factor and your growth. People need to learn what they can expect from your account to decide whether to follow you. For instance, when you think about people looking at Instagram as a form of entertainment. They are less inclined to follow an account that doesn't show up and consistently nor provide some form of entertainment. It's no value or not enough expected content for them to hang around.

Therefore, being consistent with your content gives people the indication that you will continue to post content that provides them value in exchange for their follow. In addition to showing your current and potential followers that you are active and will continue to post, it's also highly favored by the algorithms. It helps your brand recognition as you spread your footprint across Instagram.

Consistency doesn't mean you have to post 10 or 20 pieces of content per day. Consistency is finding a schedule and sticking to it for your content. The rule of thumb is to post two to three times per day. Some accounts will post more than three to five pieces of content daily, others post one time per day, and some accounts will post once every two to three days or once every week. But what we have found to be most effective with rapid growth is consistently posting every day, a minimum of two to three times. This strategy has remained true for us, and we post a minimum of two times per day. Some days, we may post three times. However, we do not over-saturate the feed with content. Posting too much content will hurt your Instagram engagement and growth. The issue with posting too much content is that Instagram sees this as spamming, and they will show less of your content when it's posting too frequently.

If you plan to post a large amount of content throughout the day, you shouldn't post content back to back within less than an hour. Posting frequently within less than an hour after you've already published a post will dramatically lessen the success that piece of content will get. For example, if you were to post something at three o'clock, we wouldn't recommend making another post until four o'clock. When you post content back-to-back within the same hour, it hurts the number of views that the post will receive.

Lastly, posting regularly on Instagram trends and hashtags makes people like you. Make them like you by liking what they like and showing up in your niche's community. As you build your Instagram following, it is imperative to be an active member of the community.

## Best Times to post

As well as posting consistently, you also need to post your content at the right time. "They say, timing is everything. But then they say, there is never a perfect time for anything." This quote from Anthony Liccione is the perfect way to explain timing when it pertains to Instagram. Timing is just as important as all the other factors taken into consideration when creating content. However, the best time to post on Instagram will depend on your audience, the type of content you're posting, and your location. There is no simple answer to this because it depends on your content and what best aligns with your audience and analytics.

You may find that your audience is more interested during a particular time of the day versus others. For example, we find that posting breakfast, brunch, or lighter meals do better in the morning than posting heavy food meals. Early content would make sense since most people will be thinking about breakfast or lunch in the morning. Also, be aware of your time zone with the content of your post. If you are located in New York and posting an LA breakfast at 5 A.M., be mindful that your targeted west coast audience is 3 hours behind you. So they might not see your content for hours, which will hurt your engagement.

When scheduling your posts, you want to be sure you know when your target audience will most likely be online and on Instagram. It helps you in judging the best time to post and engage. An app we recommend for choosing the peak times for increasing engagement is _Preview_, which gives users metrics about your following and content based on your posting history in the past.

Watching your analytics will help you judge the best time to post and engage with content on Instagram. Posting at or around the peak times recommended by your analytics will increase your engagement and likes.

## Hashtags

Use Audience-Targeted Hashtags

As we've mentioned before, hashtags are a great way to showcase your content in groups and find more people in your audience. It's also an easy way for people who post about your content to see you and vice versa. Hashtags are not the secret ingredient to "Rapid Growth" on Instagram. Hashtags are simply searchable keywords that let Instagram looking for people who posted using the keyword that you may be interested in exploring further.

Using relevant hashtags in your post is an easy way to reach people interested in the content you've shared. The best way to ensure your ability to maximize Instagram's hashtags benefits is by using hashtags that directly represent or support the details of your post and business.

Showing up in hashtags is going to be an essential part of gaining and growing on Instagram. First, you want to find the most appropriate hashtags for your business and your niche. The hashtags you use are going to look slightly different, even within the niche of food. For example, food bloggers may use hashtags like #foodblogger, #foodieblog, and #dailyeats. In contrast, restaurant owners may use hashtags like #Restaurant or #BlackRestaurantWeek. A chef could be found in hashtags such as #cheflife, #travelingchef, or #ChefsofInstagram. When you find a handful of hashtags relevant to your business or niche, we recommend following them.

To serve you well, whatever hashtags you find that best represent or fit your overall brand will be the group of hashtags you're going to want to work on dominating. As you start, we recommend making a list and finding the best 10 to 20 hashtags related to your brand business or the products you serve for ultimate growth. This way, you're able to prepare the most suitable hashtags for promoting yourself on Instagram.

Once you've located the hashtags, start utilizing these hashtags within your content and adding more hashtags specific to your post's content. Focusing on targeting a setlist of hashtags is part of what we like to call "Hashtag Domination." Hashtag domination is something we've coined because we've dominated hashtags that once before we did not exist in, and now we are at the top of the hashtag's feed.

Ideally, you want to show up in the top nine to twelve posts of a hashtag. Appearing in the leading group of hashtags will allow you to gain the most exposure when people search through those hashtags. When your post is at the top of a hashtag feed, you're seen first, noticed as the most relevant piece of content, and most likely to receive viewers' engagement.

One of the most effective ways of using hashtags is not going too broad or too small with the hashtags you are using. If you're planning to use a hashtag, such as #food, that currently has 427 million posts, understand you're more than likely going to get lost in the weeds. Overly used hashtags are not as effective as smaller to mid-sized hashtags because you're competing with millions of posts. The chances of your post landing in the top feed become very slim as the numbers of post-stack up to the millions. Also, you don't want to use hashtags that are way too specific and too small. If there is no audience in a hashtag, it won't be beneficial to use it or invest your time targeting that hashtag because almost no one will see it. Unless it's a hashtag that you are branding for your content, we don't recommend using hashtags with less than 5K posts.

## Hashtag Size Cheat Sheet

Hard / Frequent Hashtags (Broad Audience)

- Use 1-5 tags (size 1 million-5 million post)

Medium / Average Hashtags (Focused Audience)

- Use 10-15 tags (100K - under 1 million post)

Easy / Rare Hastags (Small/Niche Audience)

- Use 5-10 tags (10K - under 100K post)

We recommend a mixed usage of no more than five large frequently used hashtags, ten to fifteen mid-sized hashtags, and five to ten specific smaller hashtags. Ideally, you want to utilize rare and smaller hashtags because those will be the hashtags regardless of how big your account is. You're going to show up at the top of the feed, most likely. This allows you to gain views and smaller audiences and gain traction, allowing your content to propel into the hashtags with a bigger audience.

The sweet spot for the most effective hashtags is what you want to target the most, which are somewhere around the amount of 40K to 250K post. Smaller niche hashtags will be anything below 50,000 posts. And what we refer to as large hashtags will be anything above a million to 3 million. Hashtags above 5 million will not serve you well, as mentioned before, because there's a lot of traffic and competing posts; we recommend staying clear of these as you grow your account.

Most Instagram accounts get lost in the feed. Instagram will only allow you to use up to 30 hashtags. There have been speculations that mention using the full 30 hashtags on your content negatively impacts reach. We have not found this accurate, and we have seen no difference in the number of views we notice when using the allotted 30 hashtags.

A mistake that you don't want to make is using hashtags and then deleting them. Instagram will flag your account as they think you are trying to game the system. Do not delete and re-add hashtags. In most cases, trying to trick the algorithm will only stunt your growth. However, a tip that we recommend is going to the accounts of already successful people in your area or specific niche and taking note of the hashtags they are using.

To find the most appropriate hashtags for your business, you can use apps and online services to create a list of relevant hashtags based on a keyword search.


**Tags & Credit**

Another form of tag that will help your social footprint and growth is giving credit where credit is due. What's meant by this is tagging the rightful owners and giving them credit for their content, or highlighting products and letting people know where to find them.

For example, if you're a restaurant, and one of your customers has taken an incredible picture of your food. If you decide to post that customer's image, it's okay to tag them and say thank you. What usually happens is that the person you tagged is so happy to be recognized that they share it on their profile or story. This, as a result, then allows their followers to see your content and began to investigate your page.

As you do this more, others' followers will become aware of your page and begin to follow, interact, and share your content. Instagram also will start to recognize your content as favorable. Favorable content is then shared on the explorer page and also suggested post. The same thing applies to food bloggers by giving shoutouts to restaurants as well as food products. Helping others grow will also help your growth.

When tagging someone in a post, we recommend tagging them in the photo and tagging them in the comments.

This allows dual notifications for them to see your content as well as spreading out your social awareness. When you tag someone in a photo, you now appear in their tagged content feed, allowing people who may search that profile's tag content to find you. Tagging them in the comments section boosts your engagement. It shows the owner that you are proactively shouting them out and giving them credit for their content.

## Variety Formats (Niche, diverse)

So in the previous chapter, we talked about content creation strategy, which we mentioned using various content forms, such as photos, videos, reels, and stories. Now that we've covered how to create multiple forms of content let's look at how to grow your following by diversifying your content within your niche.

For example, I would recommend that a chef with a wide range of cooking skills and available serving, such as everything from seafood to vegan food, highlight their seafood and vegan options. The variety of degrees within your niche as a personal chef will allow you to attract a range of people by the diverse selection you have to offer. If you have multiple items on your menu, at some point, we recommend you highlight them because it brings more engagement from diverse audiences who may have an interest in certain foods.

You can still diversify your content within a niche to spread out across the area of your target audience. Remember, your niche is not food but the service you provide within the food industry.

Suppose you're posting content from one specific area or multiple particular areas within a field. In that case, you should diversify your target areas. For example, if you're a blogger covering the latest urban dish trends across the United States, you don't want to only focus on food in one area. It's beneficial to make sure you are cover more area locations. By diversifying, you are allowing your footprint to spread as your awareness grows. Because the more people in different areas that are aware of your content, the more potential new followers you can gain from the increased traffic and sharing of your content.

Diversifying doesn't mean you need to switch up your brand or what you offer on Instagram. It only means that you are putting different options on the plate, so there's something for everybody.

## Location

Location, location, location! Geotagging is one of the essential tasks that often gets forgotten on Instagram. Geotagging is the process of identifying a particular location for a photo or a place when you're posting content at any given time. Geotagging can be done in posts, as well as in stories.

Suppose your business shows up as a taggable location on Instagram. If that is so, you would want to utilize this benefit, especially if you are a restaurant owner or have a fixed location where you can do business. The reason is that customers and potential customers can find and post within your taggable location. This benefits you when someone comes across your Instagram page and looks into the geotag for your location. From that, they can see all of the people who have posted from or on that geotagging. The benefit is if you're a restaurant owner and customers have posted pictures of your food while at your location. When newcomers look at your social media page, they see what's happening at that location and the customer reviews. Business owners use this to drive more business to come to your location.

Customers who are posting from or on your geotagging act as free marketing for your service at that location. This also creates its own feed for your location. As we've mentioned previously, if you are a food blogger, the benefit of geotagging is that you can be found in these locations when posting to them. Also, it's easy to find the content of others who have been added or posted to that location. It's one of the Instagram tools that most people forget to utilize. Aside from posting to a specific address.

You can also geotag cities and states. This comes as a huge benefit because a city and state geotag typically has a massive following and post number. So, if you were to rank high within the top and recent feed for a geotagging, this would increase the traffic back to your Instagram page. Essentially, geotagging a city and state almost performances as well as a popular hashtag.

Last but not least, Instagram notifies users that you have posted to a specific location when using the location geotag. The traffic and engagement to your content also increase by Instagram telling users that you've posted. Creating content with geotagging combining with hashtags is an excellent strategy for accelerating growth and attention.

### Analytics - Who's watching?
### Find Whats working for your demographic

What is it that your audience likes? Knowing your demographics will be critical in your growth strategy. Therefore you should make the most of the tools provided to you for free by Instagram. As we have mentioned before, Instagram offers free analytic tools for business profiles. There are several ways to make the most of these marketing tools and services wisely. For example, the insights analytical tool provides you access to your likes, follows, and engagement data, plus a few other things. Of course, you may be aware of this already, but you're probably wondering how you can cash in on them. Well, insights can help you understand your audience by showing them what posts are performing well and which posts aren't. You're also able to view when you're most likely to get the most engagement. And you can find the content that seems to resonate the best with your audience by looking at what got the most likes and engagement.

Once you begin to understand what will trigger your audience's response, you can start to use this info to spark conversation and lead your followers in the direction you want them to go. Here's a little secret tip that we use. Sometimes we post things that we know will get a rise out of our audience. For example, we posted some crab cakes, which by the way, looked amazing. However, the recipe was not the original recipe that most Marylander's use. Maryland is known to have some of the best crab cakes. Crab cakes have remained a staple of the state of Maryland since the 1930s. Therefore, most Marylander's hold a certain standard and expectation of what should and shouldn't be in a crab cake.

We got a lot of responses and engagement from people from different areas across the United States, giving their opinion on how to prepare crab cakes. We knew that it would provoke people to engage and respond to it.

We knew this because we've posted similar content before, and our analytics showed the results. Engagement doesn't always mean likes, just as likes doesn't always equate to shares.

Sometimes having a little shock value within your content can engage your audience to respond more. We recommend being in a state of always trying new things. At times, you may find that trying something new worked better than anything you've ever done before. Variety leads to virality. We don't recommend only sticking to what you've done just because it did well. Please continue to reinvent yourself and re-evaluate your content to grow with the times. Innovation is key.

The content that you post will draw in your audience. And hopefully, that audience converts to followers on your profile. It's essential to be aware of the photos and videos that you use and what's working. As you study your demographics and analytics, you will become more aware of what they like and what makes them engage and comment on a post. Remember, what works for one may not be the same for every account. Everyone that's posting food will have a specific niche within the food category. So you can look at others and see what works for their content. But remember, you are your own brand, and that's what makes your content special.

## Engagement

Engage with Popular Instagrammers

One of the best ways to grow your community on Instagram is to find profiles in the same social community and niche. Community engagement with other accounts can lead to features, followers, and even being listed by IG as a "suggested follow." You should always be aware of what the most influential accounts in your niche are doing. You should pay attention to what they're doing, what's working for them, and what's not working for them.

For example, suppose you have a product that you're looking to sell on Instagram. Getting a well-known Instagrammer to feature you or your product on their feed can catapult your sales and attention. As you are aware, many people pay for this, which is called Paid Promotions or Paid Advertising. While you could pay an influencer to post your content, that's not the only way to have your content or product shared. So let's look at some other ways to accomplished this.

First, you need to find the most influential accounts in your niche. You can use Instagram's search function, which requires typing in keywords, hashtags, and company names. After finding them, Instagram will provide you with a few similar accounts "suggested for You" when following the account. These accounts recommended will typically be very similar to the one you just followed, so these accounts may also be worth looking into to boost your traffic.

Before connecting with another user, I recommend checking the person's account profile to see if their account fits your audience and their receptiveness to engage with other accounts. In most cases, you can get an idea of if the IG account accepts product reviews or supports highlighting others in their posts by reviewing their previously posted content. Plus, you might also find numerous users with a note displayed in their bio that shows their willingness to work with different companies, by lines such as "Tag us for shoutout" or "DM for Feature ." If there isn't a clear indication that a user is willing to engage with different brands, you can email them directly and ask whether they are willing to do a featured review or sponsored post for your business.

Another way we grew the Black Foodie Finder platform is by intentionally providing value to others. So, when approaching an account with a much larger audience, we didn't ask them for a shoutout. We just found a way to support or provide value to them. In most cases, they returned the favor.

Also, engaging in other users' content within your niche will drive traffic back to your page. One of the tricks we used was turning on post notifications, so we were first to comment on accounts with a huge following. We would make a genuine comment that showed that we really did look at their post. Whether the account saw us or not, the followers of that account would see our comment. That would always lead a few people to check out our content, especially if our commentary on that post caught a lot of attention.

Your popularity on Instagram ultimately lies in your hands to grab the attention of your target audience and showcase your business in the best way possible. Applying these tips will help you gain growth. While we cater this information to the food industry, these growth strategies will work for any type of account.

# CHAPTER 7

# ACTION

The ongoing popularity of Instagram will be a great way to grow your business and bring more targeted leads to your business or company site.

For many of us in this food space, growing your Instagram account isn't just about likes and follows. It's about growing your business and brand. Reaching a broader audience and touching the people you wouldn't have been able to get to without social media. For this reason, in this last chapter, we want to focus on putting everything we've discussed into action.

Now that your profile is set up with a highly effective and attractive bio describing your brand, who you are, and what you do. You are consistently posting high-quality photos and features of your staff and customers. Showing off your range of diversity and even adding music to videos that were once silent.

Your content looks excellent, your consistently posting on a routine schedule. High-quality photos of your fabulous dishes, features of your staff and customers. High Definition video footage capturing the culture and atmosphere. You're using a variety of images, carousels, reels, stories. Short captions, story captions, informing, entertaining, and inspiring your followers.

You are shouting out your supporters, sharing their content, and building connections and relationships in your niche. A link to your website, menu, blogpost, or e-book sits in your bio. And you have a call-to-action in every post. You are on your way to dominating your niche space on Instagram. You're adding value, and new followers are beginning to roll in.

Even while you don't see a massive number of followers in a couple of days or weeks, you just keep showing up and engaging with your audience and community. You've found your strategy, and you're sticking to it. If you are following all of the techniques and tips we have given, then this is you.

In the last chapter, we want to focus on action as we wrap up the book. You have everything that you need to succeed at growing your Instagram account. Now the most important thing you can do is execute. Most people with all the information and all the tools readily available yet seem to fail to start. So, with this information. I want you to begin executing as soon as you finish this chapter if you haven't already. With the information given, create a to-do list, set some deadlines, and make your most significant post. If you have not posted, make your first piece of content today. Then start strategizing on how you will continue to provide some form of quality content that either entertains, informs, or inspires your audience.

Remember, you have everything that you need. And it's all up to you to make this happen, and you can do it. You just have to do it. Thank you for taking the time to read this book. And we appreciate those who support us. And with this information.

We hope that you use it to succeed and become successful in your Instagram endeavors.

# THANK YOU

Thank you for supporting and reading this book. We hope that this guide brings you value and success along your journey. If you did receive any information from this book, please go to Instagram now and share your testimonial. Tag us @BlackFoodieFinder via your post, story or send your message to us directly.

Also, feel free to reach out to us via email and send us any success stories or questions you may have. You can reach me directly at BraxRich@blackfoodiefinder.com or our team at info@blackfoodiefinder.com.